# PRAY Without Ceasing

J. Stone

## MINDFULNESS OF GOD IN DAILY LIFE

## WAYNE SIMSIC

Saint Mary's Press
Christian Brothers Publications
Winona, Minnesota

Genuine recycled paper with 10% post-consumer waste. Printed with soy-based ink.

The publishing team included Michael Wilt, development editor; Brooke E. Saron, copy editor; James H. Gurley, production editor and typesetter; Cären Yang, designer; Pat Mutter, illustrator; hand lettering by Ivan Angelic; produced by the graphics division of Saint Mary's Press.

Acknowledgments continue on page 115.

Printed in the United States of America

Printing: 9  8  7  6  5  4  3  2  1

Year: 2008  07  06  05  04  03  02  01  00

ISBN 0-88489-668-4


Library of Congress Cataloging-in-Publication Data

Simsic, Wayne.
    Pray without ceasing : mindfulness of God in daily life / Wayne Simsic.
        p. cm.
    ISBN 0-88489-668-4
        1. Prayer—Christianity. I. Title.
    BV210.2 S535 2000
    248.3'2—dc21
                                                    99-050788

With gratitude to all the men and women

who have participated in retreats

that I have been privileged to lead

A little lifting up of the heart suffices;

A little remembrance of God.

—Brother Lawrence

# Contents

Part Two

# The Practice of Mindfulness in Daily Activity

# Introduction

Traditionally, to "pray without ceasing" was considered a practice reserved for those in religious communities, where such a spiritual discipline could be fully incorporated into a daily routine. It was thought that those who were preoccupied with making a living and raising a family would find it too difficult to integrate prayer into daily life, and that they should concentrate on finding special times to direct their attention to God.

Today, however, we realize that unceasing prayer should not be linked to a particular kind of person or vocation but to life itself. Living in a community with a shared vision has many benefits, but to cultivate an attitude of prayerfulness, we need live only an ordinary, everyday existence. Our prayer, then, becomes eating, sleeping, relating—life itself.

Doesn't spiritual growth happen in the context of everyday life? Are not the activities of working, raising a family, cultivating a marriage, juggling bills, worshiping, and fasting serious, growth-oriented disciplines? We are like the common people who came to hear Christ and then had to return to their responsibilities. By carrying out those responsibilities mindfully, can we not be drawn to a deeper faith and to unceasing prayer?

This book introduces the practice of being mindful of God's presence in daily activities. It is, in a sense, directly inspired by Paul's message that prayer is all life and therefore we should pray without interruption (see

1 Thessalonians 5:17–18). Mindfulness has become a popular term in spirituality and psychology today. It is most often linked to the practice of Buddhism, though it can be found in every religious tradition. I will be describing mindfulness in the context of the Christian tradition, but I will draw on other traditions—Buddhism, Islam, Judaism, and others—for examples.

As you read, you may find yourself nodding your head in approval, recognizing that you have been praying without ceasing but have never named your experience as prayer. Who hasn't looked at a night sky and felt a connection with God's creation, or experienced a "thank you" rise up from the depths of the heart after spending time with a loved one? I have found that many people work to keep in touch with a transforming love throughout the day, but they do not bother to talk about their spiritual discipline; they simply want to live it. Their life truly is their prayer. Others vaguely realize that life is already an interaction with God, but they have yet to wake fully to that reality.

Carl Jung built a retreat at Bollingen and had the following words inscribed in stone over his front door: "Called or not called, God shall be there." That inscription could very well be etched into our hearts. Whether noticed or unnoticed, accepted or rejected, God remains at the center of our existence, calling us. Our awakening to that truth in everyday life invites us along a spiritual path to unceasing prayer.

Part One

# Pray Without Ceasing

# 1. The Desire to Pray Without Ceasing

Do you ever . . .

- experience the nearness of the Divine at times throughout the day and want to heighten your awareness of it?
- want to claim a center of peace in a hectic schedule?
- turn off the radio or television because you value the silence?
- have the desire to extend your morning prayer into daily activity?
- find that times of prayer are not enough?
- use reminders in your car, bathroom, or places throughout the house to keep you alert to your most primary values?
- sense a need not only to say prayers but to live prayer?

If you answered yes to any of these questions, you have experienced the desire to pray without ceasing. That desire is an expression of your willingness to be open to the work of the Spirit: to want to live more in harmony with the wisdom of the universe and to participate in the fullness of divine life. We do not want to forget the Source of our existence but to remember, giving thanks and praise each moment of our life.

The desire to pray without ceasing may evolve from a daily practice of prayer or meditation. The regular practice of resting in God's presence, surrendering to God in silence, transforms us. Peace and unity found in times of prayer weave themselves into daily activity, and we experience a communion with the Divine even as we carry out our responsibilities. We grow in our knowledge that God's presence can be found in each moment of the day.

The desire to pray may also surface in the lives of those without a prayer discipline. They may find themselves repeating short prayers of gratitude throughout the day, recalling the presence of Someone Greater while in the middle of an activity, and responding with reverence to mystery in nature and relationships. However, that awareness of the Divine needs to be nurtured through a spiritual discipline that includes prayer or meditation. Otherwise it will disappear under the ebb and flow of life events and eventually be forgotten.

Paul tells us to "pray without ceasing" (1 Thessalonians 5:17). Some, however, may balk at the idea of praying always. We usually think of prayer as one activity added to all other activities. How can I find time for prayer when I am exhausted after spending a day with the family? Yet, the more we release ourselves to the flow of God's love in our life and in the world, encountering grace in surprising ways, the more we realize that prayer cannot be restricted to certain times or places. Parents with children, for example, will find that their love of and attention to their children throughout the day is their ongoing prayer because they participate in the energy of God's love. Paul, too, does not speak of prayer as part of life but as an ongoing concern; prayer is life.

We live in two dimensions—the dimension of daily activity and responsibility and the dimension of Divine Presence. As we allow our hearts to be drawn to God, we realize that we can live in both worlds concurrently. Unceasing prayer becomes a reality. The important thing is not prayers alone but prayerfulness, an attitude of prayer that weaves through the fabric of life. "Do not quench the Spirit," we are advised in Thessalonians, but "rejoice always, pray without ceasing" (see 1 Thessalonians 5:16–19).

## 2. **A Deepening Faith**

How does the desire for unceasing prayer awaken in us?
A man who lost his wife, his dear companion for over
forty years, began to pray with more fervor than ever
before. He also felt an overwhelming desire to somehow
integrate his morning prayer into his daily activity,
though he knew that would be difficult.

There are times in our life when we are called to
deepen our trust, to have faith that God is truly the center of our existence and not just an aspect of our life.
Often when we experience suffering, setbacks, unconditional love, or some significant life change, we realize
that we can no longer be satisfied with the values we
once held, but that we must turn inward with seriousness
and begin to live out of our faith.

Faith, then, becomes more than a set of beliefs to
guide us. It becomes the center of who we are. Such
faith can be described as an ongoing trust in an ever
present ground of love, a desire to remain in touch with
that love throughout our daily life, even when other
responsibilities demand our attention. While being inter-
viewed by a television correspondent, Mother Teresa
held a string of wooden prayer beads that she pushed
methodically, one after the other. What a perfect illustra-
tion of what it means to remain mindful of God's loving
presence while otherwise engaged in activity.

Our culture does not reinforce our desire to remain
in touch with a deeper reality in daily life. In fact, we are
given the impression that the human agenda is the most

important one, and that any spare time should be filled with some productive effort. Those who heard Jesus refer to the "Kingdom of God" knew of the kingdoms of Herod and Caesar. They did not fully comprehend, however, that the Kingdom of God represents a vision of the world with God, rather than any human enterprise, at the center. For Jesus, the Kingdom was a reality already at work that could be known here and now.

Appreciating the primacy of God in our life means remaining vulnerable to the holiness of the moment. It means living with our heart wide open to God's presence on Earth, trusting that God is already working in our life, inviting us, coaxing us, moment by moment.

Unless we have in some way uncovered and claimed the "kingdom" at the center of our life, it is unlikely that we will make the sacrifices necessary to embrace it and live out of it. We need to ask ourselves, When in our life did we feel the call to make the Divine central? How did we respond?

# 3. Remembering

> On my bed I will remember you,
> and through the night watches I will meditate
>    on you.
>
> —Psalm 63:6

According to a Hebrew myth, an angel comes down from heaven when a child is born, takes the child under his wing, and recites the Torah. At the end of the recitation, the angel places a finger on the upper lip of the child, creating the indentation that each human being possesses there, and says, "Forget." The child, then, journeys through life trying to remember.

This is the story of each of our lives. We forget God, and, like prodigal sons and daughters, we go off and seek our own way. Russian spiritual master Theophan the Recluse counsels: "Everywhere and always God is with us, near to us and in us. But we are not always with Him since we do not remember Him." We search for God in the far country while God waits for us at home, observes Meister Eckhart. At some point, perhaps in midlife, we wake up to the presence of Something More and attempt to find our way home.

Saint Augustine tells us that God is more intimate to us than we are to ourselves. Our being shares in God's being. Since nothing exists outside God, to forget God is essentially to forget ourselves. In Deuteronomy we are warned: "You forgot the God who gave you birth" (32:18).

The search for truth that occurs when we wake up and remember that God lives at the center of our being changes our perception of prayer. Instead of praying at given times and then taking a vacation from God during other activities, we see prayer as ongoing attentiveness or mindfulness. In that sense prayer is an attitude, a way of living. Rather than creating a corner of our life with our selves and our goals as the center, we choose to make God central.

Prayer can be described as a growing mindfulness or attentiveness to God's presence in every activity, even the most mundane, because at the same moment we wake up to divinity in the midst of work, play, or any activity, our hearts open and respond. Prayer times themselves remain important, but they are no longer segregated from the rest of our life. Instead, prayer focuses our desire to experience God's presence so that we can learn to live out of that desire amid our everyday life and activities.

One thing is certain—prayer is radical. It roots our very existence. It demands more than a partial commitment. "Prayer is the essence of spiritual living," writes Abraham Heschel. "The flow of prayer is like the Gulf Stream, imparting warmth to all that is cold, melting all that is hard in our life."

# 4. The Path of Mindfulness in Religious Traditions

Mindfulness is a common theme in religious traditions, though it can be called by other names: recollection, presence, attention, remembrance, awakening. In Islam, mindfulness is essential for awakening and realizing a spiritual presence. According to a saying by the Prophet Muhammad, "There is a polish for everything, and the polish for the heart is the remembrance of God." Sufis practice a meditation called *zikr,* "remembrance of the Divine." Buddhism holds mindfulness as a central tenet. According to Thich Nhat Hanh, a Vietnamese Zen Buddhist monk, mindfulness is an awareness of what you are doing as you are doing it each moment of your daily life. This, he says, is the essence of Buddhist meditation. In Judaism, sacred phrases or verses from the Scriptures are repeated as mantras to draw the meditator closer to God. And Native Americans consider moment-to-moment attention an essential ingredient in traditional religious life.

In the Christian Scriptures, the story of our journey homeward becomes a journey of mindfulness, or a waking up to God. God was present among us in the beginning, walking with Adam and Eve in the Garden of Eden. When the primal man and woman disobeyed, they hid from God. No longer could they enjoy divine presence everywhere and all the time; rather, they found themselves in exile.

Eventually Jesus showed us the path back to an intimate relationship with the Father. He reminded us of God's overwhelming love for us, and called us to repent, to return from exile. When we accept the invitation, we are encouraged and guided by the Spirit: "I will ask the Father, and he will give you another Advocate, to be with you forever. This is the Spirit of truth" (John 14:16–17).

Our story, then, like the story in the Scriptures, involves remembering, coming out of exile, to experience God's nearness. Paul reminds us that God is near: "In him we live and move and have our being" (Acts 17:28). No longer separated from the relationship to which we belong, we are reconciled. We trust that we live in God's presence not only part of the time but all the time and everywhere, and that awareness becomes the foundation for our ongoing prayer.

The practice of mindfulness also has deep roots in the western monastic tradition. Michael Casey comments:

> Monasticism is . . . a constant flight from mindless and comfortable routines and evasions and the cultivation of contrary habits of mind: openness to grace, sensitivity, vigilance for the coming of the Lord. Monastic regime is seen primarily as a structure of mindfulness through which the monk grows in his ability to perceive truth—about himself, about God, about the world in which he lives.

We also find mystics such as Augustine, Teresa of Ávila, Brother Lawrence, Thomas Merton, Henri Nouwen, and others calling us to mindfulness as a way to see truth.

In the end, Christians believe that Christ's conquest of death and the sending of the Holy Spirit have restored all things in Christ. What remains is for that restoration to be made manifest, particularly in the way we live our ordinary life. As Christians we should ask ourselves, Are we growing in mindfulness of God's loving presence day by day?

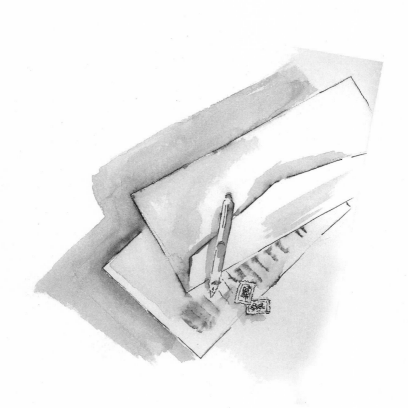

## 5. Where Is God?

If we want to pray without ceasing, we need to determine first where we find God. Is God somewhere else, not near but distant and elusive? Remember how easy it was as a child to find God everywhere—in the grass underfoot and in the wide blue sky, in churches and in our families? As adults, though, we learn to compartmentalize God. We focus on Divine Presence only in special times and holy places, effectively separating the spiritual world from common, routine reality.

We may have bracketed the divine in some corner of our life, but we still long to hear a whisper calling to us in the middle of our ordinary routine. Brother Lawrence, a Carmelite lay brother, heard that whisper in Paris in 1666. As a former soldier and household servant, Lawrence found God in the kitchen more often than in any other place, even the church. He did not separate work from prayer, but insisted that he remained in God's presence no matter where he was or what he did. Jesus himself encourages us to pay attention to everyday life. He uncovered sacredness in common things and actions—a mustard seed, wine, bread, cleaning, mending, baking. He did not segregate experiences, but saw all reality as alive with possibility.

Sometimes life-changing experiences rip away images of God that we have clung to since childhood. A woman who lost her mother expressed her anger toward God, believing that God had betrayed and abandoned her in a time of great need. After a few months, however, she realized that her suffering had stripped away an image of God that she had become comfortable with—the image of a distant, authoritative, grandfatherlike God—and introduced her to an intimate yet transcendent God who walked with her in the darkness.

One lesson we learn repeatedly from the mystics is that we should not reduce God to our own expectations. We need to be open to sheer mystery, to the fiery love that can engulf us. Like Moses before the burning bush, those who suddenly realize God's nearness experience an "aha" moment. Wide-eyed and gasping, they stand stunned by the knowledge that they are so completely loved. I remember a woman who found herself grasping for words and could only say that she was "in Something Greater." She repeated the same phrase again and again with a tone of wonder and awe. Those of us who listened to her felt as if we too had been encircled by an intimate love.

Many struggle to believe that God truly loves them. They may take up addictive behaviors, or spend a lifetime searching for someone or something that will prove to them that they are loved. All the while a quiet voice waits patiently in the depths of the heart, whispering but remaining unheard. Once we wake up to the truth of God's love, we realize that it will never abandon us and that it flows abundantly like so many rivulets through every part of our experience. We realize we have done nothing to deserve that love but, nevertheless, we are truly gifted with it and should be called children of God.

While working in Canton, Mississippi, during the civil rights struggle of the 1960s, psychiatrist Robert Coles talked with a black man, Joseph Gaines, who offered this description of where he found Jesus:

I'll be praying to Jesus, and I'll feel Him right beside me. No, He's inside me, that's it. . . . He can be your friend all the time, not just Sunday morning. Come Monday and Tuesday and through the week to meet Him in church, or go find Him some other place—He's everywhere, if you'll only want to look. If you live with Him long and hard, you're carrying His spirit; if you think of Him but once a week you're just another—I guess you be another Mississippian!

This example of how primary and graced our awareness of the nearness of God is reminds me of a story. Once a young fish asked an older one where the water was that everyone talked about. Rather than describe water and confuse the younger fish, the older fish simply said, "Keep swimming." For a person who has not yet experienced the intimacy of God and the need to pray always, there is not much we can do; we can only say, "Keep breathing."

## 6. Simple as a Glance

Our difficulty with prayer can often be traced to our tendency to complicate it. We cannot imagine unceasing prayer because we think prayer is complex. As a result, we feel guilty that we are not praying in a certain way or often enough. We read about prayer, but we only come away more confused. In short, we make prayer our issue and forget that it is God's work. We forget that prayer is primarily a gift of the Spirit.

Prayer is also simple. God is already present. We need only pay attention. If we truly trust in the intimacy of God's presence, our mindfulness of that loving presence is our prayer. Thérèse of Lisieux describes prayer as "an upward leap of the heart, an untroubled glance towards heaven, a cry of gratitude and love which I utter from the depths of sorrow as well as from the heights of joy." Brother Lawrence would agree. He says, "I keep myself in His presence by simple attentiveness and a loving gaze upon God."

Stuck in the rut of trying to pray in a "proper" way, feeling guilty that we do not pray often enough, or convinced that we are not the kind of person who prays, we forget that the presence of God is as near and as simple as a glance. Like a child who runs to find a parent, looks into her or his face for a moment, and then runs away, we glance toward God during the day and are reassured and healed. Thérèse of Lisieux reassures us that even when we fall asleep at night, we are embraced, like a child, by our loving Parent.

We don't have to manufacture intimacy with God or even take time to think about God's presence. In fact, thinking will get in the way. Intimacy was present from our birth. We simply have to discover that spark of eternal love at the center of our being. Our response should not be complicated but should be a simple gesture of love, a glance in God's direction. But more than being a passing look, that glance extends from the heart and gathers together all our humanness, including emotions, desires, thoughts, and senses. It may lead to a conversation with God, a sense that Jesus walks with us, or the desire to rest in God's presence. But initially, and more important, the glance is a surrender to infinite love in the midst of the ordinary.

We are reassured knowing that our glances and wordless sighs are a form of prayer. Paul assures us in Romans that "the Spirit helps us in our weakness; for we do not know how to pray as we ought, but that very Spirit intercedes with sighs too deep for words" (8:26).

## 7. A Matter of the Heart

> When you search for me, you will find me; if
> you seek me with all your heart, I will let you
> find me, says the LORD.
>
> —Jeremiah 29:13–14

What is the key to simple prayer? The heart. In ancient
tradition the heart represents all our humanness gathered
together in our longing for God. Today, however, we are
very "head oriented," so we have difficulty connecting
with the heart. An active mind supersedes the heart.
When we experience more head than heart, we should
bring our thoughts from our head to our heart. In the
words of the Russian mystic Theophan the Recluse, to
pray is to "descend with the mind into the heart, and
there stand before the face of the Lord, ever-present, all-
seeing, within you." In that way we are not ignoring
thoughts but integrating them with our deepest concern.
Eventually our thoughts will mesh more easily with our
longing for God. We will not feel that they must command our whole attention.

The following story from the Jewish mystical tradition dramatizes the importance of heartfelt prayer:

> An angel told a rabbi about a man in a distant
> city whose prayers were most pleasing to
> God. So the rabbi set out to find the man. He
> reached the city and searched the House of
> Study but could find no one who knew the
> person he was seeking. He went to the market-

place, and when he inquired he was told that the man was a poor farmer who lived in the mountains.

The rabbi journeyed into the mountains until he came to a small hut. The poor farmer greeted him. The rabbi put aside his astonishment at the poverty of the surroundings and immediately got to the point. He asked the farmer to tell him the secret of his prayers. The farmer, with a surprised look on his face, replied, "I cannot pray, Rabbi, because I cannot read." The rabbi asked, "What did you do on Yom Kippur?" The farmer responded: "I went to the synagogue, and when I saw how intently everyone was praying, my heart broke. I began reciting the letters of the alphabet, asking God to accept these letters and make them into a prayer for me. I repeated this with all my strength." Immediately the rabbi understood that this man's prayers were precious to God because they came from the heart.

The anonymous author of *The Cloud of Unknowing,* a classic mystical text from the medieval period, gives brief instructions for the prayer of the heart. The author suggests focusing on a word like *God* or *love* or some other one-syllable word, and linking it to your heart. That word, then, becomes an instrument of love that the heart uses to push aside distractions and penetrate the darkness of ineffable Mystery. "I pray you, then, to follow eagerly after this humble stirring of love in your heart. It will be your guide in this life, and will bring you to grace in the next."

How do we know when we are not living out of a heart center? When we no longer feel contentment in God, and when our compassion for others falters. Jesus promised, "Blessed are the pure in heart, for they will see God" (Matthew 5:8). Purity of heart flees when our own agenda and excessive self-concern muddy our awareness; the heart becomes unsettled and anxious.

Perhaps we should look to children for examples of heart-centeredness. I remember watching a child on Cadillac Mountain in Acadia National Park. Seeing the beautiful vista for the first time, the child let out a cry of delight and stood completely focused, his eyes opened wide in wonder—a full-hearted response to the present. The adults who accompanied the child were preoccupied, talking about the difficulties of driving to the top of the mountain, pointing to landmarks they recognized, and planning the day ahead. They failed to sink into the wholeness of the moment, to forget themselves and their concerns, and, at least for a moment, to re-engage the heart.

In the Christian tradition, beginning with the desert fathers and mothers and including countless holy men and women, purity of heart requires cleansing ourselves of all poisoning influences such as narcissism, restless distraction, and the persistent need for control. Purity of heart, Danish theologian Søren Kierkegaard reminds us, is to will one thing. Our lives become pure when our energies are channeled in a single direction and not diverted by an inner neediness. Centered on God alone, we embrace more of life itself, not less, because we are no longer divided, burdened, or pulled apart by confusion and unnecessary concerns. We begin to honestly enjoy God's presence, like a child enjoying a majestic vista, and in turn we allow God to enjoy us.

## 8. The Sacredness of the Now

What are you doing now, this moment? Reading? Day-dreaming? Bring your attention to the present, be awake to this reality: In this moment God is greeting you. To be mindful, to be in the moment, we must encounter God, who is present now.

Being mindful of the nearness of God day by day uncovers surprising holiness. We sense mystery in the sound of rain tapping on the roof as we fall asleep, in the smell and taste of an early morning cup of coffee, in the fragrant scent of a morning breeze, in the sound of a friend's voice, in the touch of a person we love. Those are everyday, ordinary moments, but they suddenly cata-pult beyond the common and reveal themselves as gifts. We find mystery in the ordinariness of a squirrel in the backyard or a flower leaning in a breeze, and we know something profound has occurred.

"Remove the sandals from your feet," God told Moses, "for the place on which you are standing is holy ground" (Exodus 3:5). Each common place, each ordi-nary moment, is holy. Yet, most of us are like Jacob who, when he woke up, said, "Surely the LORD is in this place—and I did not know it!" (Genesis 28:16). Imagine the molecules of the universe held in existence moment-by-moment; all life, including our own, supported by a loving Presence, without which all beings would disap-pear. From that perspective Paul's claim rings loud: "From him and through him and to him are all things" (Romans 11:36).

Our willingness to remain open to the present depends on our trust. Are we able to hand over our control, our insistent need to direct our lives, and let God's will become our primary concern? Are we open to letting go of wounds from the past and anxiousness about the future to trust in a Presence greater than ourselves? Do we choose to fill the moment with our own agenda, or are we willing to rest in God's presence? Even in moments when we feel nothing and our mind goes blank, we can choose to simply rest in the spirit of God.

Jesuit Jean-Pierre de Caussade assures us that "we can find all that is necessary in the present moment," and that we should strive to carry out God's purpose not only this day or this hour but this very moment. By accepting that counsel and trusting God, we are released from our feverish desire to manipulate the events of our lives; finally, we can relax. Nothing else matters but to respond to the will of God in the present. The "will of God," however, does not refer to an external force that imposes rules and restrictions but to an invitation to truth and love that comes from within each moment. To ask ourselves whether we are acting according to God's will is to be alert to the invitation to truth and love now. What is God asking from me in this present situation?

Each moment rises up like a seed, and no one knows how (see Mark 4:26–27). Creative love is working, and each day holds promise. It is easy to take for granted that mysterious germination and growth of the now, but those who are wise learn to treasure it. A

Hasidic tale relates that after the death of a revered rabbi, one of his disciples was asked, "What was most important to your teacher?" After a short time the disciple replied, "Whatever he happened to be doing at the moment."

Recall some of the events of the past day and ask yourself: What was being asked of me in those events? What small miracles have I been aware of this day? Sinking deeper into the present, into the revelation of the here and now, we realize that prayer cannot be limited to time and place but is an ongoing response to the sacred. Surrendering our heart to God moment-by-moment is our prayer.

## 9. The Art of Attention

According to a traditional Sufi tale, a man dies and finds himself in front of a slowly revolving door. A voice tells him that every thousand years the door opens into paradise. He should pay attention and enter when it opens. As time passes, the man watches the revolving door. Then a thought distracts him, perhaps a memory of his life on Earth, and the door opens for a moment and then closes. The man misses it and must wait another thousand years.

This story represents how much is at stake if we forget to be attentive. The period of a thousand years symbolizes the enormous loss that the man suffered when he failed to remain open to the moment of revelation. He bartered eternal happiness for the sake of distracting thoughts or illusive desires.

In the Garden of Gethsemane, Jesus, "deeply grieved even to death" (Matthew 26:38), asked his disciples to wait nearby. They tried to stay awake and keep watch, but they fell asleep. Jesus asked, "Could you not stay awake with me one hour?"(Matthew 26:40). Twice he asked them, and twice he returned to find them asleep.

When Jesus asked his disciples to keep watch with him during his anguish at Gethsemane, he did not want them to perform heroic actions, solve problems, or save him from threatening circumstances; he asked only that they wait and be attentive. In their humanness, Peter, James, and John fell asleep. They were unable to respond to a request that seemed simple but was, in fact, very difficult.

We, like Peter, James, and John, soon discover how difficult simple attention can be when we try to be present to someone in need—a friend, for example, who is grieving or dying. Nothing is demanded from us at those times except to just be there, still and watchful. Activity no longer matters; all that matters is presence and attention. So we sit, feeling inept, unpracticed in the simple art of attention. Gethsemane teaches us that perhaps the most simple and yet profound thing we can do at times like those is to stay awake and be present.

## 10. **Cultivating Attention**

We may decide to be attentive to God's nearness during times of prayer or during everyday activity, yet we find that our mind quickly wanders; it flickers, dances everywhere, like a flame in a breeze. Denise Levertov asks:

> How can I focus my flickering, perceive
> at the fountain's heart
> the sapphire I know is there?

Attentiveness is a serious and necessary discipline. As a nineteenth-century Russian Orthodox teacher said, "Without attention there is no prayer."

The wandering mind cannot be completely harnessed. By nature it pulls off in one direction after another, at one point mulling over past failures and hurts, and, at another, imagining future ambitions and opportunities. It rambles on even when we are thinking of nothing in particular, and it continues to work as we sleep. We wake up with memories of dreams still floating in our consciousness, and realize how active the mind has been through the night. It seems we are always thinking. How, then, can we turn our attention to God's presence?

One possible answer is that instead of thinking about other things, we restrict ourselves to thinking only about God. But thinking about God all the time is impossible, not only for people with many responsibilities but even for those who have few. Daily routines and responsibilities call for our dedication and attention. Even if we were able to spend several hours in prayer every day, we still would not be able to think about God all the time. Human nature would not allow it.

A wandering mind, though, need not be considered a distraction; it can be, instead, an invitation to gently shift our attention back to the present and the presence of God. Rather than trying to control the mind's meandering, we bring our thoughts, fears, all our emotions and dreams, before God. We find that conversing with God or simply enjoying God's presence becomes part of the rhythm of our lives. No matter how we feel, what we are doing, or who we are with, God remains present, a constant in our daily existence. We live and think centered on God, and we return to that center again and again. We no longer need to perpetuate the illusion that we have to turn away from the activities of daily life if we are to be with God.

Without God in sight, our lives flounder. With an attachment to God, our lives find anchor in meaning and hope. Jesus himself lived his life in complete openness to his Father. He did not hide his joy, fear, hope, and despair from his Father, but shared everything. His example leads us away from a self-oriented life to an ongoing relationship with God. Reading the epistles of Paul, we get the impression that Paul himself lived and wrote in God's presence, for Paul frequently moves in and out of prayer. To live and think in God's presence throughout the day is to possess the courage and faith to live not in privacy but in relationship with Someone greater than ourselves. Our lives then, become prayer.

At first it is easy to dismiss the idea of praying always because it seems like we already have too many things on our mind. We ask ourselves, How do we bring God into an already crowded life? However, as we have seen, God is not an addition; God is already present. We need to open our lives to that Presence again and again, to think and live in the Presence that knows us better than we know ourselves. The more we remember that we are not alone but that we live in dialogue with God, whether we are conscious of it or not, the more we understand unceasing prayer.

# 11. Making Room

> Human ways are under the eyes of the LORD.
> —Proverbs 5:21

I recall a teacher from my early years telling the class, "God always watches you, and you should always try to do your best." That instruction struck fear in my heart at the time; I pictured God waiting around every corner, and I was unnerved by the loss of privacy.

If we truly believe that God sees us in every place and knows our thoughts, would we not be transformed? Would not that awareness bring a new quality to our lives?

Perhaps we do not believe that God is present everywhere and sees everything. If that is the case, for the sake of more mindful living, we need to strengthen our conviction that we do stand before the eyes of God. The theme of God's watchfulness can be found in both the Old Testament and the New Testament: "The eyes of the LORD range throughout the entire earth" (2 Chronicles 16:9); "Your Father . . . sees in secret" (Matthew 6:4). Even our innermost thoughts are subject to God's scrutiny: "Yahweh, you search me and know me. . . . You perceive my thoughts from far away" (Psalm 139:1–2).

At first the omnipresence of the Divine may strike fear in our heart, but remember that a loving God knows us more truly than any human being can, and more than we know ourselves. Our only desire, in the end, is to be transformed by that love.

Authentic transformation calls us to let go of all that separates us from God. We are invited to lay our brokenness before God, to surrender more and more to the love we uncover at the center of our life. Holy men and women know that truth, but so does each person who begins the spiritual path with seriousness. "Draw near to God," says James, "and he will draw near to you" (James 4:8). We cannot keep a part of our inner life hidden and secret and apart from the sacred. We are called to an ongoing conversation with God that includes the whole self and every aspect of our life.

We can think of ourselves, metaphorically, as a violin created from the finest wood, yet meant to be hollow so that beautiful music can resound in and through us. Our strings are tightly wound, which can cause tension and pain, but it is through them that we can create beautiful music in the hands of the Artist.

But allowing music to sound in the depths of our life, to live in the presence of God, is very difficult. Perhaps we shield ourselves from God because we do not want God to know our dark secrets and wild fantasies; we think that God cannot accept that part of us. Or we do not want to let go of the private pleasures that we have come to depend on. To show them to God would mean that we would have to release them. In the end, unceasing prayer eludes us because we refuse to bring our life into a divine light. Rather than open our heart to an abiding Love, we stubbornly choose to resist. In the end, that disobedience leads to illusion and despair because, in essence, we are rejecting the very reality of our life.

Those who wake up to the underlying movement from self-consciousness toward God-consciousness feel strongly that their lives are changed irrevocably. They realize that they are called to their greatest happiness. No longer satisfied with a monochrome life, they allow God's loving presence to color their sense of self, their hopes and dreams, and their relationships. They offer their lives as a clean canvas, and they trust the painting to the Artist.

## 12. In Times of Stress

Becoming mindful of God's presence in our life can be a challenge. It is one thing to be attentive to God in quiet, peaceful moments, but what about the busy or hectic times? How do we pray unceasingly in the middle of chaos?

The pager is beeping, the phone is ringing, and a doctor enters the office without knocking. A social worker in a cancer center of a large city hospital rifles through papers on her desk, searching for the phone number of a patient she forgot to call yesterday. She catches herself and realizes that she is becoming more and more frustrated. She stops everything, taps a gong at her desk, breathes deeply, and relaxes. Having touched a peaceful center for a few seconds, she resumes work. Nurses and visitors ask her about the gong. She smiles and taps it so that they can hear the resonance and take a moment for themselves.

Each of us needs a way to remind ourselves of God's presence in this moment, even if we are surrounded by busyness or chaos. In fact, the more we open our heart to a peaceful center in times of crisis, the more we realize that the crisis itself can be an occasion for growth and that prayer weaves itself through our life. What we perceive in the beginning as an impasse, a heated exchange with a coworker, for example, can reveal itself in time as an opening to self-knowledge. We see that the context of this moment is greater than we thought. Not only does the moment surprise us, it invites us to deepen our awareness of the mystery of every moment of the day.

## 13. Breath of Life

Mindfulness can be retained during demanding situations through attention to breathing. For example, a hospice volunteer, aware of the mystery and sacredness that surrounds her encounters with the dying and their families, stops for a moment before entering a room, breathes deeply, and asks the Spirit for help. By attending to her breathing, she becomes aware of life within and around her. Nothing can hold her back—she is free. She is able to accept the event as it unfolds, let go of all that distracts her attention from what is most important, and remain in the presence of the spirit of God.

The prophet Ezekiel, along with the Jews, believed that the breath of life comes directly from God: "'Thus says the Lord GOD: Come from the four winds, O breath, and breathe upon these slain, that they may live'" (37:9). The wind was seen as God's life breath, God's spirit. Our breath or spirit shares in the life, the breath of God. To breathe deeply, then, can be an act of faith, putting us in touch with the Source of life. For many traditional religions, such as Buddhism, Hinduism, and Islam, to meditate is to breathe; and to breathe is to detach ourselves from trivial concerns and allow our life to be drawn back to Truth. In Sufism, for example, cultivating and refining the breath is a method for surrendering to the divine presence each moment.

A fundamental way to remain mindful of God in the middle of any situation, then, is to attend to one's breathing. To forget is to find oneself short of breath, rushed, controlled by outside circumstances; in other words, to be removed from the Source of all life. Take a moment now to center yourself through breathing.

When you connect with your breathing, you may at times find yourself repeating a word or phrase as you breathe. For example, you may be gardening, and a few words from a psalm will come to mind; or, during the ride home from work, you might say "Into your hands," "Help me," or "Thank you" as you think over the day. You repeat a phrase naturally with the rhythm of each breath. The simple phrase seems to express all you need to say at that moment, and you recite it inwardly again and again. The author of *The Cloud of Unknowing* assures us that God prefers the simplicity of short prayers that express the heart's longing. What a relief to pray with the rhythm of breathing and trust that God knows our heart!

## 14. **Other Ways to Remain Mindful**

We should take advantage of the times and activities in our schedule that invite mindfulness. For example, an office worker might practice mindfulness during an early morning jog before work, or during a walk at lunchtime. An elderly person who has difficulty eating with utensils might choose to practice mindfulness while using a spoon. A gardener might be drawn to mindfulness while gardening. Too often we search for unique or special avenues to the Divine when the most potent spiritual path is found in the ordinary events that draw our attention.

Another common way to practice mindfulness involves retreating to a particular place to pause quietly—a garden bench, a window, a chair in the study, a quiet room, a path in a local park. We may also find ourselves alone and mindful while traveling to work or school, resting as the children sleep, raking leaves or cutting grass, gardening, or performing some ordinary household task. And we can practice mindfulness while eating an apple, washing clothes, taking a shower, standing in line at the supermarket, walking, putting on our shoes, or getting dressed.

The sweet scent after an early morning rain, the smooth surface of a flower petal, the texture and warmth of a hand, the smell of basil rubbed between the fingers, the taste of warm apple pie, the words of a favorite song—all these sense experiences, because of their immediacy and mystery, call us to mindfulness. If we truly believe in the Divine center of our lives, then each of those experiences expresses the energy of God. Everyday sensory experiences, including the expression of our bodies during times of joy and sadness, introduce us to the potency of the present and the riches of the inner life.

Do you enjoy playing the piano, hitting a baseball, writing a poem or a journal entry? Those are all mindful practices that call you to be where you are in a special way. What activity creates enthusiasm in you, makes you feel alive? Have you considered that to be your practice, your graced time?

Finally, because it is easy to become immersed in the events, thoughts, and feelings of a particular day, it is helpful to incorporate "triggers" to call ourselves to the practice of mindfulness. For example, think of small activities that you perform every day—taking your first bite of food in the morning, turning on lights, watching television, turning on a car radio, picking up the phone, stopping at a red light. Or create your own unique reminders. A woman has a sign hanging in the bathroom with the word *Yes* on it, so that she remembers to say yes to the goodness of the day. Each time I see a hummingbird at the feeder, I remember that the moment is graced.

When a trigger occurs, stop long enough to recollect the sacredness of the moment. Step aside from the flow of time and sink into the now. Simply be. You will return to your responsibilities refreshed and with a renewed vision. The power of those short moments of recollection is amazing, and we carry over the inner freedom and tranquillity we gain from them into whatever we do. We pray without ceasing.

## 15. **We Breathe One Breath**

After a period of silent prayer in a large group, a woman commented that she had an awareness of all those in the room breathing the same breath in unison. She said that even though she knew few of the people in attendance, and even though she realized that each person had his or her own unique breathing pattern, she experienced one common breathing.

It is tempting to think of mindfulness as a private practice, as one's personal way of finding peace in a hectic schedule. In fact, there is no such thing as private prayer. "'Private prayers' is a misleading phrase," writes Br. David Steindl-Rast. "First of all, true prayers are never private. . . . Genuine prayer comes from the heart, from that realm of my being where I am one with all." Because God is one, and we choose to live in God, then we will discover ourselves united to all life, including all creation. Prayer is primarily a participation in the prayer of Christ himself and of the whole church. Prayer as a member of the body of Christ happens not only during time set aside for prayer in the morning or evening, in church, or in nature, but also when we practice mindfulness throughout the day. Remembering that helps us keep our prayer from becoming too self-concerned and forgetful of God and our neighbor.

Prayer that remains private constricts the soul, binds it with ego concerns. It produces lethargy and depression. Authentic prayer gives us strength to reach out to others with compassion. It expresses itself in a deeper love and commitment to Gospel values and social mindedness. How can we be fully present to the Divine here and now and ignore a situation in which the dignity of a human being is being stripped? Mindfulness heightens our sense of justice. It calls us to be prophets, to stand up for what we believe, even if it means standing alone against group opinion.

Even while reading a newspaper or watching the news, we do not escape our engagement with others. We see tragedy and cruelty through our awareness of God's presence in all events. We cannot view the news of war or senseless killing passively; it is a call to pray that God's will be done and that justice prevail. In so doing, we participate with a world that cries out for redemption in the middle of chaos.

We should pray, then, that through the Spirit we can transcend our anxiousness and fear, and that we can unite with all the members of the family of creation, especially those who are suffering and dying, and with wounded Earth herself:

*God of light, lead me to the center of my being.*
*In peaceful attention let me become aware that*
*I am in communion with all other human be-*
*ings, with nature and beauty and the goodness*
*of all that is.*

## 16. Ways of Prayer

"Be still, and know that I am God."

—Psalm 46:10

What form of prayer do you use on a daily or regular basis? Have you found that a particular form of prayer or meditation practiced regularly has deepened your sense of the divine throughout the day?

Without a regular prayer discipline, the idea of unceasing prayer will eventually dissipate in the push and pull of everyday life in a contemporary world. We need to create fertile ground so that the seeds of revelation have a chance to germinate and poke through the thick crust of daily routine. Growth in the discipline of unceasing prayer demands setting aside time for prayer. Many forms of prayer are possible—personal, communal, liturgical, devotional, and contemplative. But we need to take time to praise and give thanks, to give glory to God alone; then we will find a growing capacity to pray always—to remember God's presence throughout the day. Perhaps the most startling example of that occurs when we hit a rough time and feel completely lost and isolated. Surprisingly, in the darkness, we receive an assurance that we are protected and cared for. Our prayer has continued even though we have forgotten it.

After the Apostles had completed their duties, Jesus told them to "come away to a deserted place all by yourselves and rest a while" (Mark 6:31). Jesus often retreated into the silence of the high mountains or desert so that he could be alone with his Father. He knew that silence was essential to the continuation of his work. In the same way, the silence we cultivate at particular times gives us the courage to stop in the middle of a busy schedule and dive within, beyond the surface tension of immediate concerns. It strengthens faith, preserves inner peace, and creates more time and energy to look deeply into ourselves and find a perspective for helping others.

The following prayer forms offer ways to remain open to the present and thus extend prayer into daily life: the Jesus prayer, centering prayer, *lectio divina,* and the liturgy. Let us take a closer look at each of them.

## The Jesus Prayer

*The Way of the Pilgrim* is a charming tale of a Russian peasant who, while walking through Russia, prays the Jesus prayer. His experience becomes a guide for anyone who feels a compelling desire to enter into the "heart" and learn how to pray always. The Jesus prayer transformed the pilgrim gradually. He writes:

> When about three weeks had passed I felt a pain in my heart, and then a most delightful warmth, as well as consolation and peace.
> . . . Sometimes my heart would feel as though it were bubbling with joy; such lightness, freedom, and consolation were in it. Sometimes I felt a burning love for Jesus Christ and for all God's creatures.

With practice, the Jesus prayer can grow like a germinating seed, become self-activating, and enter the rhythm of your breathing and the beating of your heart. Take a few minutes to experience the prayer and see how easy it is to synchronize it with your breathing. Voicelessly repeat the words of the Jesus prayer, *Lord Jesus Christ, have mercy on me,* for five minutes. Integrate the words with your breathing: *Lord Jesus Christ* on the in-breath, and *have mercy on me* on the out-breath. Find a rhythm that feels natural and allows you to focus on Christ's presence. You may eventually adopt another form such as, *Lord Jesus Christ, you are light; fill my mind with peace, my heart with love.*

If distractions occur, simply let them go and bring yourself back to the prayer. It is also important to be patient with yourself and to repeat the prayer during times of prayer and throughout the day. Let the memory of Jesus take root in your heart, and let the name *Jesus* become as intimate to you as the name you breathe. In time the prayer will become a powerful way of anchoring yourself in the moment, and will often rise of its own accord before you are conscious of needing it. Remember this promise: "Those who love me will keep my word, and my Father will love them, and we will come to them and make our home with them" (John 14:23).

## Centering Prayer

Take a moment and focus on the Holy Spirit dwelling in the depths of your being. Do not give in to the compulsion to say or think anything in particular. Simply be in the presence of the Spirit.

This is the beginning of centering prayer, a prayer method taught by spiritual writers such as Thomas Keating, Basil Pennington, John Main, and others. In the stillness of resting in the Spirit, you awaken to a center of peace. Distractions flow through your consciousness like debris on the surface of a river, yet you release them while repeating a sacred word such as *Jesus,* and allow yourself to be drawn back into the presence of God.

Centering prayer is a simple prayer, but it can be quite difficult in the beginning. We are pulled in so many directions during our daily life that to remain in the presence of the Holy Spirit can seem truly foreign to our experience. With practice, however, we find a center of quiet that we can carry with us throughout the day. More than an occasion to be present to God, centering transforms our day and awakens us to creative love in every aspect of our life. Those who center themselves discover greater self-knowledge and a changed relationship with people, with their work, and with creation. They truly become more vulnerable to the Divine in their daily routine.

Thomas Keating offers these suggestions as ways to bring centering into daily life: nurture a genuine compassion for yourself, carry a book of short readings that you can refer to during in-between times, and practice allowing other people to be who they are rather than trying to change their behavior. Other suggestions, as well as an introduction to centering prayer, can be found in Keating's book *Open Mind, Open Heart.*

## Lectio Divina

Welcome with meekness the unplanted word.
—James 1:21

Reflecting on the Scriptures day-by-day makes the heart more open to God's presence and more aware of its dependence on that presence to stay on course. When we open our heart to the nourishment of God's word, we feed our soul and we remember to live according to ultimate values rather than becoming lost in less important issues. According to the Desert Fathers:

> The nature of water is yielding, and that of a stone is hard. Yet if you hang a bottle filled with water above the stone so that the water drips drop by drop, it will wear a hole in the stone. In the same way the word of God is tender, and our heart is hard. So when people hear the word of God frequently, their hearts are opened to the fear of God.

If God's word is to have an effect on our life, we cannot simply read the Scriptures as we would read a magazine article. The monastic practice of *lectio divina* invites us to ponder the word and to receive it into our heart. We need to read slowly, stop at passages that speak to us, relate the word to the events of our own life, and attempt to put the word into practice. In this way the word gradually opens our life to God's presence in the middle of daily events.

While reading the Gospels, concentrate on being present to Christ with all your senses and your whole being. Reflect on Christ's image—as healer, spiritual guide, teacher—in the passage. Listen to what Christ is saying to you, and enter into a conversation with him. You can take that image and that conversation with you into the day. When you have a quiet moment, return to it, and let the image become the silent witness to your thoughts and activities.

Take time to read the Scriptures each day for a week. Read slowly, meditatively, allowing the word to catch your attention. God speaks to you here and now. Stop at a word or sentence that addresses your particular circumstances, and reflect on it in the context of your life. Open your heart to the Good News, and let it inform your daily life. Let the Gospel story be a safe haven for you during the busy and difficult times, and transform those times into prayer.

Finally, choose a short phrase or word that appeals to you, and recall it throughout the day, letting it shed light on your present activity. In this way the word drips, drop by drop, on a heart immersed in daily events and opens it to the presence of God.

## The Liturgy

In the liturgy we discover true mindfulness of the presence of Jesus Christ as Lord, Savior, and Risen One. Like the pilgrims on the road to Emmaus, we recognize him in the breaking of the bread:

Then their eyes were opened, and they recognized him; and he vanished from their sight. They said to each other, "Were not our hearts burning within us while he was talking to us on the road, while he was opening the scriptures to us?" (Luke 24:31–32)

The community responds to the command of Jesus: "Do this in remembrance of me" (Luke 22:19). In the Hebrew context, remembrance was not merely recall but a sense of being present to past events, specifically to the Last Supper and to the dying and rising of Christ. The community gathered in the name of Jesus is a sacrament of the presence of Jesus.

The eucharistic community gathers to listen to the word of God, to rejoice in the presence of Jesus, to forgive and love their brothers and sisters, to share in the body and blood of Jesus, and to carry out the mission of the Holy Spirit. A eucharistic Christian continues to be mindful of the presence of Jesus in daily life. The eucharistic celebration spills out into a eucharistic life where trials and tribulations, broken promises, and broken relationships test us. Do we live the eucharistic celebration? Do we really become "living Christs"? Can we indeed say that we have met him on the road? Having been nourished by the body and blood of Christ, we are mindful of ourselves as ambassadors who follow the command and blessing, "Go in peace to love and serve the Lord."

## 17. Fruits of Praying Always

As we learn to extend prayer into our daily life, we find that our inner geography changes. We retain a center of peace and love more readily in the midst of daily life. We gain a quiet confidence in God's work and play through us, and we are less intent on controlling life circumstances. The beauty of life, the simple forms of nature, the common pleasures such as the taste of food, the warmth of the sun, the coolness of shade, the rhythm of a heart, and the awareness of being alive capture the soul. In fact, we imagine our entire being as an expression of divine love.

We also learn that our life is not our own, that we are children of God trusting completely in a divine Parent. As a result, we experience a new freedom, an openness to wonder and playful participation in the life unfolding around us. Each moment is alive with divine possibilities, is surprising, is a miracle. The child comes alive within, and we see from the heart. In short, we answer Jesus' invitation to "become like children" and find revelation now.

A heightened awareness of the abundance of the Divine each moment inspires a deep sense of gratitude. Br. David Steindl-Rast insists that mindfulness cannot be separated from gratitude. And, indeed, how can we experience the dynamism of love welling up each moment, creating and re-creating our lives, and not respond with a thankfulness that spontaneously rises from the depths of the heart? How can we continue to pray our lives without mindfulness that all life depends on God?

Grateful living brings peace, says Thich Nhat Hanh. When we are grateful due to mindfulness, he says, we are peaceful, and if more people were grateful there would be less violence in society. That makes sense when we consider that those who give and those who receive come together, creating a bond between them. Thich Nhat Hanh speaks of "being peace," or being in a state of at-one-ment with others, which can sometimes lead to reconciliation. That gentle monk's dedication to peace reminds many of Francis of Assisi.

Finally, joy, more than any other sign, characterizes true prayer. The recurring effort of the heart to recall the silent center, the mindful reordering of one's life toward God, can seem like drudgery over time. Yet moments of insight unfold when we perceive the boundlessness of God's love. As a result, hope and joy enter the soul, supporting and reassuring it. Setbacks still occur, but now they are reminders of our dependency on love, and they become occasions for growth. Joy, and the hope that naturally accompanies it, impels the heart to greater transformation.

Take a moment to remember the signs of divine love in your life. Choose some way to celebrate the joy and hope you have experienced—laugh, sing, shout out, dance, create, live out of that unimaginable joy in whatever way inspiration draws you to.

> You will show me the path that leads to life;
> your presence fills me with joy,
> and your help brings pleasure forever.
>
> (Psalm 16:11)

Part Two

# The Practice of Mindfulness
# in Daily Activity

# 1. The Sacredness of the Ordinary

Let us now focus on growth in mindfulness during the course of an ordinary day. Through attention to our daily activities, we awaken to the presence of God in the moment and discover that our life is prayer.

Growth in mindfulness means more than numbering the times we remember God. It evolves into a heightened awareness of the loving kindness of God that was always intimately present but was habitually ignored. Mindfulness, then, is not an exercise in concentration but a posture of the heart, an attitude of trust in God's presence within every activity.

Focusing on common, everyday activities allows us to remain grounded in concrete experience and avoid the illusion that spirituality is removed from ordinary life. Focus on the everyday also allows us to retain a perspective on what is most important in a world characterized by busyness, noise, and technological innovation. Washing clothes or gardening in a mindful way, for example, may be simple acts in themselves, but they stand as strong contradictions to a consumerist society that encourages spending and acquiring more products.

It is important to begin the practice of mindfulness in comfortable stages. We may choose to set aside one day a week in which we can practice mindfulness in every activity rather than to attempt mindfulness for an entire week and become frustrated; or we might choose to select one everyday activity and perform it mindfully for a week. Retreats and even vacations can offer opportunities for a more concentrated practice of mindfulness.

Most important, we need to remember that mindfulness cannot be rushed, because God is working in us, and we will progress in God's own time. We enter this practice knowing that deepening our intimacy with God will not happen overnight but will involve a lifelong journey.

In the pages that follow, we will focus on mindfulness during the ordinary rhythm of a day: waking up, eating, working, walking and other leisure activities, enjoying nature, forming relationships, and preparing for sleep. Pick and choose suggestions that will heighten your own awareness of the Divine. Attend to those and let go of the rest.

Begin this exploration into daily mindfulness by thinking of times when you are aware of God during the course of an ordinary day.

## 2. **Waking Up**

What is the greatest difficulty you encounter when you get out of bed? Are you already in a bad mood before you put a foot on the floor, overwhelmed by negative thoughts and feelings? Do you tend to entertain that negative energy as you prepare for the day ahead? Do you rush through your morning rituals, all the while preoccupied with other concerns?

The Christian tradition calls us out of spiritual slumber and into the light of Christ. To begin the day mindfully, we need to ground ourselves in that light. Instead of letting negative thoughts and feelings take over, we should pause a moment to remember that we are reborn each day of our life into the embrace of God's love. Though the day may be difficult, and at times we may feel like we are losing ourselves, we stand secure in the belief that God loves us unconditionally.

At the beginning of each day, we should see ourselves as children, dependent on a nurturing God who loves us unconditionally, healing and transforming us. Recall God's promise: "Can a woman forget her nursing child, or show no compassion for the child of her womb? Even these may forget, yet I will not forget you" (Isaiah 49:15).

### Morning Rituals

It is important to take our time with morning rituals. No matter how small or insignificant the ritual seems to be—brushing teeth, putting on shoes, combing hair—we should give it our attention. By anchoring ourselves in the present, we release our attachment to intrusive thoughts and feelings. They drift into the background as the ritual becomes our entrance into the sacredness of the moment.

Rituals are an occasion for enjoyment and gratitude. Taking a shower and feeling the warm water refreshes body and soul. Water cleanses and removes our sleepiness. We slowly sip a cup of coffee, smell it, enjoy it, rather than swallow it quickly for a caffeine boost. Being present to a simple pleasure like coffee at the beginning of our day introduces us to ourselves. We find a moment to be aware of our life. Watching the sun rise, reading the paper, taking a morning walk—all these morning rituals can be an occasion for joy.

Most mornings we remain on automatic pilot, but it is surprising how one simple activity done with mindfulness can alert us to what we really desire in our life and can rinse away some of the day's anxieties. We may also awaken unexpectedly to our profound giftedness. One woman describes a transformation that came over her as she dressed. Putting on shoes and socks, she was overcome with an appreciation of her feet. She stopped a moment, acknowledged them, blessed them, and continued dressing.

## Time for Prayer

All religious traditions stress the importance of prayer in the morning. Morning is seen traditionally as an ideal time for prayer because we are not yet preoccupied with the day, and we possess an inner calm. The discipline of drawing aside to a sacred place allows us to immerse ourselves in divine love. The form of prayer can vary widely—reading the Scriptures, sitting in silence, walking, or a simply lighting a candle. Most important, this time of prayer represents a gesture of love in response to God's abiding presence in our life.

Teresa of Ávila admitted that early in her calling she stopped praying because she felt she wasn't getting anything from it. Later she regretted her decision. She realized that prayer is not primarily our time but God's time to act in us. Even if distractions overwhelm us and the act of prayer becomes dry, we believe that, in some hidden way, our life is being transformed and, moreover, that we will be given the strength to continue our prayer during the day.

But what happens when we forget or run out of time? One day a cobbler asked a rabbi for advice on that very topic. He found himself working most of the night and through the morning. As a result, he often missed his morning prayer. When the rabbi asked how he was coping with the situation, the cobbler answered:

> "Sometimes I rush through the prayer quickly and get back to my work—but then I feel bad about it. At other times I let the hour of prayer go by. Then too I feel a sense of loss and every now and then, as I raise my hammer from the

shoes, I can almost hear my heart sigh, 'What an unlucky man I am not able to make my morning prayer.'"

Said the rabbi, "If I were God I would value that sigh more than the prayer."

Guilt that results from lapses in attention or missed times of prayer should not distract us from the real issue, which is our desire for God. Instead, we should get in touch with the heart's sigh for God throughout the day. We cry out: God, I long for you, increase the fire in my heart. Those "sighs too deep for words" (Romans 8:26) are the seeds of prayer without ceasing. When you wake in the morning and a thousand distractions crowd your attention and you are running out of time, take a moment to get in touch with your desire for God. Offer to God all that is passing through your mind. Let your growing consciousness of the day expand to include a presence greater than your individual concerns.

# 3. **Eating**

The Japanese tea ceremony pays a great deal of attention to the preparation and drinking of tea. A relationship between tea drinking and the inner life evolves in the ceremony through the practice of mindfulness. As a result, the ritual imparts a deep peace to the participants, an inner calm that continues into the world and helps buffer the small setbacks of daily life.

The tea ceremony triggers questions about our relationship with food and drink. Do we see a connection between food and the inner life? Have we experienced being fully present to a meal and then carrying the feeling of peace and gratitude into other activities?

## Consumerism

Today we have difficulty retaining a primary relationship with food. We have little connection with the growing and processing of food. Products show up on supermarket shelves, and we buy them and consume them.

While cultivating the family garden as a boy, I toiled in the sun, hoeing and pulling weeds. I sensed the companionship of green plants, smelled ripening vegetables, buried my hands in mounds of dark loam, and felt the hot smooth skin of a tomato next to my cheek. The garden experience heightened my appreciation of food and my own mysterious relationship with it. I easily imagined a direct connection between the miracle of growing things and my own life energy.

We cannot all live in agricultural communities, but by growing even a few tomatoes or plants in a backyard or on a windowsill, we can resurrect a sense of reverence for food and its relationship with us. We may even begin to crave more purity in what we eat, to abstain from highly processed foods, and to concentrate on fresh vegetables and fruit, especially produce we can buy locally.

## Food as Spiritual Nourishment

The more attention we pay to food, the more we realize that it is related to us on deeper levels than consumption. Eating has a spiritual dimension; food nourishes our soul. By eating mindfully we find that we are changed in ways other than the physical.

Noticing that his friend was so immersed in a problem that he was popping slices of tangerine into his mouth without paying any attention to what he was doing, Thich Nhat Hanh suggested to the man that he try eating one section at a time. Immediately the friend woke up and realized how inattentive he had become. Commenting on his friend's process, Thich Nhat Hanh wrote: "It was as if he hadn't been eating the tangerine at all. If he had been eating anything, he was 'eating' his future plans."

We often use food as an emotional crutch and eat in an unconscious trance. Our inattention to a meal leaves us hungry for more. We eat but remain unsatisfied. When is the last time you ate with a quiet mind, focusing your attention on your food and truly experiencing the act of eating? Recall recent occasions when you were unaware of eating because your mind was elsewhere.

When we slow down and pay attention to eating, we enter into the most fundamental and rewarding relationship we can have with food. Eating with awareness can be practiced each day with minimal effort, but the experience brings unimaginable joy and satisfaction. Take time to savor the food, to rejoice in it. Pay attention to the way it makes your body feel. Also, do not limit your appetite to the food but take in the entire experience: the ambience, the conversation, the aromas, the company.

A simple experience can often reveal much about our relationship with a deeper self. Select an orange, an apple, or a tangerine and separate it into sections. Close your eyes. Breathe deeply until you are relaxed. Open your eyes. Look at the food and sense your desire for it. Smell it. Take one section at a time and concentrate on the experience of eating. Take time to enjoy and wonder as you eat. What did that process tell you about your inner life?

## Thanksgiving

To reinforce our spiritual connectedness to food, we can reflect on its journey from the earth to the table. The sun, rain, and earth nurtured it; people collected and processed it; a cook prepared it. Now, with respect and gratitude, we pay attention to the food we eat, savor it, and remain centered in the moment. True appreciation and thanksgiving rise spontaneously from such mindfulness.

When a family gathers for a meal and gives thanks, it mirrors the community that comes together to celebrate the Eucharist, believing that Jesus lives among them. The word *Eucharist* means "to give thanks." Meals that highlight the centrality of God's presence, then, have an inherent power that can transform the lives of all who participate.

Meals today are often quick and superficial. We have lost much of our ability to celebrate with food and drink. Because we are unable to share love and friendship around a table, we have difficulty putting our full attention into the celebration of the Eucharist. Consider for a moment the atmosphere that surrounded the Last Supper, when Jesus celebrated with an intimate gathering of friends. Now ask yourself in what way you can enhance the quality of your meals. Perhaps you can form a habit of giving thanks before eating, even at a fast-food restaurant.

## Cooking and Sharing a Meal

Another way of practicing mindfulness in relation to food is to prepare a meal for others. Put yourself completely into the process and refocus your attention when it wanders to anything else. Through your mindfulness you offer others a gift greater than you can imagine.

In the movie *Babette's Feast,* Babette, an accomplished chef, escapes the chaos of her homeland and finds work with two sisters who lead a small religious community. Babette's talent with food remains hidden until she wins the lottery and decides to spend the entire prize on a feast for the sisters and their community. At first the community is unappreciative, even presuming that the sumptuous feast must be a temptation sent by the devil. As the meal progresses, though, the members are overcome with compassion for one another and ask forgiveness for past grievances. They laugh and sing and eventually join hands in a circle to share a hymn of joy.

## Fasting

There is another way, perhaps a surprising one, in which we can improve our relationship with food, and that is through fasting. Many people are not aware of the positive aspects of fasting. They see it primarily as a tool for losing weight or as an ascetic discipline that means little in today's world.

A one-day juice fast, though, can give us a more objective awareness of eating. Afterward we are more alert to the tendency to consume food mindlessly. When we break the fast, we taste food as if for the first time. The natural flavor of an apple, a banana, or an orange, for example, comes alive in our mouth after a fast.

Fasting also wakes us up to our inner life. By temporarily paying less attention to food, we reconnect with a deeper hunger. Instead of being led by desires, we see that we have the freedom to live our life according to an ultimate sense of truth. Through the ages holy men and women fasted not because they disliked food or wanted to inflict pain on themselves, but because they wanted to stay connected with the love that they found within.

# 4. Working

Usually we think of work as the dull, routine part of our life. We identify with the plight of Adam and Eve when they were banished from the garden and had to work by the sweat of their brows. Work becomes punishment even though we may reap rewards like prestige and financial gain.

Because we don't accept work as part of our "real" life, we try to escape it by looking forward to the weekends or taking long vacations. We live for the time when we can leave the workplace behind and enjoy ourselves. To see work that way, though, is to forget that it has a wider meaning. We do not work just for ourselves and our personal goals. We work with God toward a new creation. That may sound vague, especially in an individualistic culture, but our work has a deeper significance that is built into the nature of creation. We are meant to work for a purpose beyond ourselves, for whatever we do, no matter how seemingly insignificant, carries importance because it is woven into God's own work.

The connection between work and prayer, work and mindfulness, becomes clearer when we consider that no matter what work we do, it is sacred. Every task, no matter how mundane, furthers God's creation. We do not work alone but as cocreators with God. That unique vision transforms all we do.

# Mindless Activity

We can easily lose ourselves in activity and forget the center of our being. I sit at the computer and write. In time I become frustrated that the writing is not going as smoothly as I would like it to. As a result, I force myself to write better, and when the results are not forthcoming, I become even more frustrated until the writing process grinds to a halt.

We throw ourselves into our work and become like a fire that has lost interest in burning because it is concentrating on its smoke. Such mindlessness forfeits the inner peace that comes from knowing and being grounded in God: "If you seek him, he will be found by you, but if you abandon him, he will abandon you" (2 Chronicles 15:2). We need to find our true selves, not in the whirlwind created by our busyness but in the depths of the soul, the origin of all our actions.

We must act, but our actions should reflect a peaceful center, not the anxiousness of those trying to justify their existence through activity. To make that point, Meister Eckhart uses the image of a hinge on a door. Though the door moves back and forth in its daily activity, it remains anchored on an immovable hinge. The hinge represents the center of our life, where we contentedly dwell in God.

If we remain mindful of that center, our actions will reflect the peace and love we find there. We will not think about when we will be finished with our work or what we will do when our task is completed. We will respect the rhythm of prayer and work and appreciate the moment as given.

## Approaches to Mindful Work

Even in the midst of a chaotic work environment, we find grounding in the present by using a mantra or by simply attending to our breathing. We may not feel anything at the time, no sudden awareness of inner peace, but we trust in God's presence even if we do not witness that presence.

In time the practice of mindfulness in difficult circumstances will strengthen our faith. We will have an easier time turning inward whenever we choose to. Also, we may be surprised to find that good things can come out of the chaos. A situation that at first appears detrimental to physical and spiritual wholeness could facilitate hidden growth because it offers the opportunity for needed change or self-reflection. At the very least, an impasse forces us to pay attention to ourselves and to make decisions about our priorities.

We can also remain centered by putting ourselves completely into our work. We need to give what we are doing our full attention. The best examples come from manual work. As I chop wood, I can feel the pull on my muscles, my grip on the ax handle, and the impact of the ax head on the wood. My entire body becomes fully involved in the flow of the activity. If my attention wanders, I risk hurting myself. Washing dishes, reading a book, driving a car—all these activities call for our full attention.

However, a problem arises. We usually think that giving our full attention means furrowing the brow and trying as hard as possible. Such effort is often counter-productive. Simone Weil, in an essay on studying, tells us to give our attention to the task at hand in such a way that we do not impede the activity itself. Participate in the activity; do not try to manipulate it. I remember trying so hard to loosen a frozen bolt that I broke it. Rather than stand back and look for creative ways to approach the problem, I created an even larger problem. Often the way we handle little jobs reveals the way that we approach greater work responsibilities.

Mindful that we do not work alone, we nurture the awareness of God's presence at the heart of our activity. We learn to give ourselves so completely to the work we are doing that we leave no room for self-satisfaction or letting the mind wander. We stack wood not only to have wood for winter but simply to stack wood and be in the moment. We learn to be present to God, here and now, in faith and love; whenever we are distracted, we gently return to that presence. That is prayer. We are simply "all there," doing what we are doing. The Shaker tradition puts it simply: "Hands to work, hearts to God."

Finally, we may discover that certain tasks, such as cutting the lawn or cleaning the house, engage us fully because we enjoy them. As a result, they easily become avenues of prayer. A woman who felt overwhelmed with the thought of her father's terminal illness put on rubber gloves and began cleaning the kitchen from top to bottom. As she gave all her energy to the task, she found herself speaking aloud to God and stopping at different times to weep.

Finally, as Brother Lawrence suggests, we can take time to pause and remember God while we are working. Brother Lawrence himself disliked working in the kitchen. But he believed that God was present in every one of his tasks, so he made a practice of lifting his heart to God in the middle of his work and thus performed his duties well. We find the spirit of that simple Carmelite lay brother echoed in Thich Nhat Hanh, who advises that we wash dishes to wash dishes and not rush through the task to do something more pleasant.

Even if we forget God's presence or go for long periods of time ignoring God, Brother Lawrence advises that we should not chastise ourselves, but instead turn our attention to the abundant love in our life with even greater appreciation and trust. Above all, he suggests, trust God's nearness, ask for strength, and even demand grace. Short acts of remembrance during everyday activities increase our mindfulness and give us a center of peace even in the busyness of life. Peace waits everywhere for those who practice simple attentiveness.

## Ordinary Activities

Catherine de Hueck Doherty, an exiled Russian aristocrat who fled her native land after the revolution, dedicated her life to working with the poor and the homeless. She founded Friendship House in Harlem, New York, in the 1930s and Madonna House in Ontario, Canada, in the 1940s. She grounded her spirituality in the Gospels and taught her followers to live in God's presence by diligently attending to the moment and doing even the smallest tasks well for the love of God. She realized that to live in God's presence we must be mindful, fully recollected, during our ordinary life. Otherwise life will lose meaning.

Following that prescription for living, we perform ordinary tasks thoughtfully and with full attention, understanding that they are miraculous in their own way. Eventually we discover a generous and caring God, a God who does not want to confuse us or complicate our existence, but who simply wants us to live deeply and to embrace everything we do.

While the house is quiet, a young mother rises and prepares lunches for her children. With each sandwich, she recalls the faces of her children and takes delight in them. After they awaken she guides them through their routines and out the door to the bus stop. She waits with them and kisses them good-bye as the bus approaches.

For a mother who sees the face of God in each member of her family, the ordinary morning ritual of nudging children off to school becomes prayer. Even the simplest routine, when performed mindfully, becomes a prayer that overflows with abundance of love for all. We need to trust that all our labors bear fruit because they are done in cooperation with God's plan. In our work we serve others, and can even offer our labor for those who are suffering. To imagine that we work in isolation is to ignore that all humanity, and the universe itself, is journeying to a new creation.

## 5. Walking and Other Leisure Activities

A good friend mentioned to me how much she loved to watch baseball. She said that she could lose herself in the game and forget everything. She was surprised when I mentioned that such complete attention to the moment could be her prayer. If watching a baseball game allowed her to forget herself and remain open to the drama of the event, which in itself was an expression of divine energy, then her participation could be her prayer.

We usually think of gardening, walking, reading, listening to music, and other activities as ways of shedding the weariness of everyday routine. But they can be much more. By losing ourselves in those activities and giving them our complete attention, we touch a divine center in our life. We are literally transformed by the activity. In some grace-filled moments, we may even taste a bit of heaven on Earth because the experience so completely transports us. Recall the image of Eric Liddell in the movie *Chariots of Fire*. Liddell, a runner and missionary, felt God's pleasure when he ran. As we watch his legs and arms, his entire body, respond to an inner rhythm, we can see that he is transported.

## Sabbath Time

A woman takes a pottery class and finds that the class not only teaches her an art form but gives her an opportunity to center herself. A man walks his dog after work and releases the tension of the day. He favors a path along a river, and thinks of it as sacred space. A woman works in a garden or takes a cooking class to strengthen her spirit and to balance the demanding responsibilities of her work.

The Creator worked for six days and rested on the seventh. We, too, need Sabbath times throughout the week, and not only on a particular day, to refresh ourselves and to reconnect with the goodness of our life and the world around us. These times remind us that we are not limited but creative. We draw our energy from Someone greater than ourselves.

Sometimes grace surprises us. For example, we may experience an enveloping light and warmth as we work in the garden, a moment of insight into the truth of our life as we read, or a sudden sense of oneness with the ball and the court as we play tennis. It is a taste of paradise on Earth, the way that God sees the world. If we are honest, we realize that we return to those activities because they have the potential to open us to the eternal in time. We realize that in our own creative play, we participate in the divine play of the universe.

As we experience Sabbath times throughout the week, we can participate in our daily routine with a new vision: All time is sacred. Sabbath is not the opposite of routine; it is the ground and depth of routine. The whole week, Monday through Sunday, is God's time, and we are invited to live in it. That vision may become cloudy as the days pass, but the taste of being in touch with Someone greater than the self stays with us.

# Walking

We walk by faith, not by sight.

—2 Corinthians 5:7

For many, walking inspires mindfulness. Sometimes those who walk practice mindfulness without knowing it. They walk with joy, get in touch with their bodies, and find great pleasure in the world around them—trees, birds, the contour of the landscape, the light reflected from city buildings, the warmth of the sun, the smell of a breeze. They never thought of walking as prayer, yet they experience both the intimacy and the joy of divine energy when they walk.

To walk mindfully, forget instructions and walk naturally without doing anything or going anywhere in particular. In other words, don't let your head take over and make walking a chore. To walk mindfully, simply walk. Think of Thoreau's description of walking as sauntering.

Often you will find yourself walking too quickly, as if you need to get somewhere or to appear purposeful. Slow down. Let your movement reflect your awareness of God's presence. Walk in a way that allows you to listen, to be attentive. If your arms jerk about and your gait is awkward, surrender your hurry and tension to God. Take deep breaths, relax your shoulders, and walk.

As you walk, eventually bring your attention to the rhythm of your breathing. Do not change your breathing, simply notice it. When you are comfortable, synchronize the rhythm of your breathing with your steps. For example, inhale for three steps, then exhale for three steps. Let yourself become familiar with that rhythm. If you cannot pay attention, you are walking too quickly.

Next, shift your attention to your body, to the way your weight shifts from one foot to another, to the way your foot lands on the ground, to the feel of the ground underfoot. If you find yourself leaning too far forward, pull back. If you are walking too stiffly, relax. Let your body bring the news to you.

After you feel comfortable in your body, your attention spontaneously shifts outward. If you truly relax in the moment, you will find that people or nature will greet you. You will notice someone's face or a particular tree. You may even be drawn to a particular place because it speaks to you. Continue to walk, and allow your encounter with people and nature to create itself.

Sometimes we are surprised by revelation. A man told me that on his walk a certain tree caught his attention. As he rested under its boughs, his senses became more acute. He felt fully alive, present in the moment, sensitive to the warmth of the sun on his face, the texture of bark against his back, the fullness of the sky and the thickness of the earth. A hidden energy buzzed around him. He imagined that he had been re-created and was experiencing nature for the first time.

Ultimately, walk as a pilgrim who trusts in God. Walk, not looking for anything in particular or with anticipation about where you are going but as one guided by faith, trusting that meaning will unfold in time. Like

Abraham, take a risk and believe in the promise that God offers you. Walking in that way, you uncover a deep sense of freedom and joy; you become open and alive to yourself and to the world.

Now go and take a walk.

# 6. In Nature

Many of us today put a significant distance between ourselves and the natural world, making the world a backdrop and nothing more. We do not routinely participate in or engage the world around us; we are accustomed to acting on nature, manipulating it so that it suits our needs. We are more prone to clear land for a housing development than to create a park where people can enjoy trees, plants, and streams. Nature is mostly an object for us, not alive and responsive.

Through mindfulness we find that nature is far from dead. It lives and reaches toward us. Just as we sometimes gesture toward nature, nature gestures toward us: We see the lake, and the lake sees us. We encounter a deer, and the deer reaches out to us. We no longer imagine ourselves isolated, walking around in an uncaring environment, but we see ourselves intimately connected to the natural world, as if we belong on the planet. We pray a rose and pray a finch because we see life energy flowing everywhere. Everything in creation becomes a companion, offering life to us. We may not be able to explain that connection to others, but, nevertheless, we know it exists. We are healed, and we cultivate a sense of harmony by remaining awake to it.

## With the Eyes of a Child

Mindfulness of nature begins by returning to a childlike gaze. As children we could simply stand and look. Anything could absorb our complete attention. As adults we lose our sense of mystery, and our concentration becomes scattered. Adults often run around doing several things without having a sense of wholeness. Many would agree with Abraham Heschel's observation that our information age has neglected the value of simple wonder. "The beginning of our happiness," Heschel asserts, "lies in the understanding that life without wonder is not worth living." We collect bits of knowledge and link them together, but our being remains fragmented. However, standing still in wonder gathers together the whole person.

We never lose the ability to wonder. Jesus asks us to become like children. To reconnect with the child within us does not involve regression or childishness but rather a spiritual maturity. We see creation, so to speak, as God sees it. In the words of Nikos Kazantzakis:

> Truly, nothing more resembles God's eyes than the eyes of a child; they see the world for the first time, and create it. Before this, the world is chaos. All creatures—animals, trees, men, stones; everything: forms, colors, voices, smells, lightning flashes—flow unexplained in front of the child's eyes (no, not in front of them, inside them), and he cannot fasten them down, cannot establish order. . . . Chaos must have passed in front of God's eyes in just this way before the Creation.

Through the eyes of wonder, we recover our playfulness and our prayerfulness. In prayer we might think about God or look for new spiritual insights or ideas. A deeper form of prayer, however, draws us into a heightened awareness and love for God—a playing, dancing, and praying in response to a world of mystery. We wake up to the mystery of being, and explore its depths. Mind and heart become one with what is seen; the distance between the seer and what is seen disappears. Attention becomes prayer.

This form of prayer can occur not only in our encounter with nature but through drawing, writing, contemplating works of art, participating in liturgy, or gazing at the face of a loved one. We are all seers who have been given the gift to perceive things in depth, and in so doing, to discover our true identity.

Take the time to gaze at something common—a stone, a leaf, an apple. See more than an ordinary object; see with the eyes of faith and let that small piece of creation reveal its depth. At first there will be distractions, but give yourself time to calm down and trust in the process. Eventually, if you gaze long enough, you will see something more appear, a horizon against which the object stands out. You will see what you are gazing at as part of a greater context, supported by the Source of all life.

The Creator, vibrant with life, constantly pours into the cosmos, into our own soul, and into the smallest part of creation. Should we not participate in that creative expression by extending ourselves in mindful love toward each part of creation? We may find ourselves moved to cry out to a gracious God:

For all these mysteries—
for the wonder of myself,
for the wonder of your works—
I thank you.

(Psalm 139:14)

## Harmony and Giftedness

When our eyes are opened and we are mindful of God's love in the world around us, we will feel at home on the planet and in the cosmos. Outer and inner worlds will no longer seem separate but will be seen as part of an underlying harmony that flows through the universe. Such awareness reinforces feelings of wonder and awe. Thomas Berry says that we participate in a liturgy celebrated by the cosmos itself. We join birds, flowers, seas, mountains, animals, and stars, all singing of the divine.

A sense of giftedness also flows out of mindfulness. We appreciate that the world is not ours, we did not create it. In fact, the world receives its dignity from the Creator, and we need to respond with respect and reverence for each member of creation.

Francis of Assisi once advised a brother who was planting a garden to preserve the wildflowers and let the grass grow wild around the border because the wildflowers praise God in their own way. He chose to respect the sheer giftedness of nature apart from human involvement. He believed that creation gives glory to God without any help from us.

When we see a flower, we can choose to be mindful of it as an expression of the divine. Instead of picking it, we can let it remind us of the divine abundance of life everywhere and offer it for the benefit of all living things. Through the practice of letting go and learning to receive creation as a gift, we shed our pedestrian view of the world. We practice resting in the present and uncovering a sacred ground that encompasses all life. We live out of prayerful awe and wonder.

# 7. In Relationships

On the way to a camping vacation, my van suddenly lost power on an interstate highway. When I was unable to restart the vehicle, I quickly became disheartened. I saw no sign of civilization for miles, only acres and acres of farmland. I climbed over a fence and embarked on what I thought would be a long and fruitless trek. In a short time, though, two men in a state maintenance truck pulled up and asked if I needed a ride. I told them my story, and they said they knew a part-time mechanic who lived a short distance away. I squeezed into the cab, and we were off.

We arrived at a farm, and a retired couple greeted us. The man told me that he couldn't help me because he was unfamiliar with my vehicle. But he offered to call a local dealership in the morning. The couple insisted that I stay the night, and led me to their son's empty bedroom. (He was away at college.) At dinner we talked, laughed, and shared a simple meal. I felt completely vulnerable, overwhelmed by the knowledge that, as a stranger, I was being treated with courtesy and kindness. That night I fell asleep with a deep sense of gratitude, confident that I was cared for in more ways than I could imagine.

I have learned that when we release our own concerns and expectations and simply respect the presence of people, we are often surprised by the outcome. We all have to depend on other people at some point in our life: lost keys, unemployment, sickness, a stalled car.

When the couple showed me such generous hospitality, I had a sense of all humans related as brother and sister. Of course, relationships are complex, and joy often comes with a strong dose of frustration and pain; yet on occasion, when we get out of the way, a relationship has a chance to become a surprise. We may even learn that love has the magical power of uniting people in unexpected ways.

## A Prayerful Center of Service

As we become aware of how much God loves us, we will see signs of that love in people and in the world around us, and we will reach out to others. If we do not believe that we are loved, then we will see others and the world as being against us. Reaching out to or being in the presence of others, then, will be very difficult because we would feel that we have nothing to give and will receive little in return.

Take a moment and think of the good in yourself, the values by which you live. Think of the goodness that you extend to others in a variety of ways, perhaps without thinking. Our service toward others flows from our mindfulness of love in our selves and in the world. The sign of that is our spontaneous response: a smile or greeting to another, our willingness to extend a hand to someone in need. As we breathe, we breathe in the love of Christ. As we exhale, we offer that love to others. The Spirit within encounters the Spirit in another.

A nurse intuited that an elderly man who had not had any visitors was close to death. She went to his room after her shift and sat with him for an hour, holding his hand. The next day she learned that the man died shortly after she ended her visit with him.

The nurse's simple act was a tremendous example of mindfulness in her service toward others. She spontaneously responded to someone in need with an act of love. She sensed that the man would die, and she became his companion for the final stage of his life journey. Likewise Mother Teresa acted with mindfulness in her care for the dying. She offered each a gift of love so that they could die with dignity.

Service that is not mindful of those being served quickly becomes self-serving or an extension of one's inner confusion. It is service solely for the purpose of ambition or gain. Such service cannot be considered an act of love but as an extension of a personal agenda. Actions performed with mindfulness have a dynamism of their own. Food offered or a helping hand extended in mindfulness opens the door for grace that transforms both the giver and the receiver. Christ shines through the activity and produces in it a deep joy.

## Fruits of Loving Mindfulness

As the practice of loving mindfulness grows, we will be released from the grip of anger and hatred, as well as from the tyranny of negative thoughts. We will be able to understand and accept others more completely, and we will express love and joy more spontaneously. Like a summer rain, love will penetrate the ground of our lives, softening it, making it richer and more fruitful.

Mindful of God's presence as we talk with others, we listen more intently to their needs. Instead of half listening, waiting for a chance to speak, we retain an openhearted, nonjudgmental attitude toward others; in other words, we extend hospitality. We remember that each person is a deep mystery to be explored and appreciated. We may even feel moved to pray for others. Conversing with a friend in need or a stranger who is weighed down with sadness, we focus on who that person is and what that person is saying, and find ourselves bathing that person in divine light. When we take time with people in this way, we see them as Jesus saw them, and we create a safe place for them to reveal themselves. The Buddhist practice known as *metta* also emphasizes looking for the good in others, and extending our heart to strangers, offering them a wish for their well-being.

When we are mindful of God's presence, we will also be more interested in radiating peace to others. Peace, according to Francis of Assisi, must be cultivated in the heart before it is offered to others. Throughout his life Francis practiced remembering the love of Christ, dedicated his energy to conforming his heart and mind to the will of Christ, and prayed for transformation. As a result, he discovered the ability to proclaim peace to all, whether human being or creature.

Ask yourself, Did I offer an inner peace to others today, or confusion and anxiety? Practice greeting people in a way that shows that they deserve love and respect. When you pass a stranger who catches your attention, silently wish him peace. By practicing that loving attention toward others, our heart expands and we discover an enormous capacity for love. We will also find that gestures of love begin to flow more spontaneously from our heart.

## Detachment

Loving mindfulness, however, has a price: detachment. We act for the sake of another and not for our own expectations. We do not let ourselves become frustrated when someone does not choose the path we wish for them or for the relationship. A doctor can hope that a patient will follow advice, but if the patient ignores the advice, the doctor must let go. Parents want what is best for their children, but must give them room enough to make their own choices.

To truly love, we need to learn how to be in the presence of another in a way that helps that person be the person she or he is meant to be. We listen not to direct someone's life but to respect the work of the Spirit. That is no easy task. But mindfulness teaches us to draw back when we become too absorbed. Without mindfulness we will inevitably stifle a relationship by imposing expectations on others—expectations that they may be unable or unwilling to fulfill. When that happens, others become overwhelmed by our presence, not inspired by it.

A powerful example of detachment occurs when we accompany the dying on their journey. The Buddhist practice of cobreathing can be a way of prayer at such a time. The practice of cobreathing, a way to intimacy through the sharing of the Spirit (the original meaning of the word *spirit* is, in fact, "breath"), involves adjusting our own breathing to the general rhythm of the person who is dying. It allows us to accompany the dying in a way that is nondirective but attentive to unconditional love.

# 8. **Preparing for Sleep**

Finally, we look at the mindfulness of preparing to sleep. We can become amazingly inattentive as the day ends. We scurry around trying to complete projects; we watch television, jolted by the mayhem depicted on the evening news; we eat late and get into conversations about the difficulties of the day. All of those activities, rather than settling us and helping us move toward sleep, energize us. We act as if the day will continue endlessly.

As children we avoided sleep in any way we could, begging for one more glass of water, one more story, or playing with brothers and sisters well into the night. As adults we practice avoidance as well. We sleep when we are too exhausted to do anything else.

Evening can be a quiet, contemplative time. It is a time when the body naturally begins to settle, when reading or listening to music soothes the soul. As shadows grow longer, thoughts rise to the surface and we can relax in the day's end. Evening shelters us like a blanket; we pull it around ourselves slowly, moving inward as we do so.

## Spiritual Practices

We prepare for sleep by moving inward at the end of the day. We choose activities that enhance the settling of mind and spirit, like reading and listening to music. It lets children see that as the day comes to a close, we need to grow quiet and calm, attentive to the time for sleep. No doubt this may seem like a losing battle, but children will eventually take the cue from their parents.

We can also close the day by incorporating an examination of conscience, a review of the day in the presence of God. With a nonjudgmental attitude, we bring to mind the events of the day, and we observe our thoughts, feelings, and actions in terms of how God seemed to be present in them and how we responded to God's presence.

An examination of conscience may be difficult for some. For example, I learned in grade school that an examination of conscience meant a relentless search for sins that were committed that day. I concentrated on good and bad actions, thinking that God preferred to hear about those selfish moments and not about my times of pleasure and play. I finished my examination feeling defeated. No wonder I shied away from the practice.

A different approach is to move from self-inquiry to discernment. Instead of listing sins—with the childlike hope that we will not die in our sleep—we invite God to be with us as we recall the day. In God's company we sort out the day's activities. We can grieve over our careless actions or the times we willfully turned away from God, but we can also rejoice in discovering the gifts we received and had little time to acknowledge in all the busyness. Most of all, we begin to see an underlying pattern and direction in our life; we come to know a hidden hand directing it. Eventually, with a regular examination of conscience, by inviting God into our life again and again with a generous and open heart, we will begin to recognize God in all things and become aware of a deep current of love throughout the day.

Perhaps the reason we do not continue with that form of examination is that we soon find out that we are not who we thought we were. We uncover a net of our own attachments. We imagined ourselves free, but we realize that we are, in reality, bound by distractions and desires. However, through a regular examination of conscience and God's mercy, we begin to know ourselves and to overcome obstacles along the inner path. We begin to know the "I" as the inner God, Christ within. Daily attention to our life teaches us to let go of all that we have been or hope to be, to face each moment with our true identity in Christ, open to whatever comes.

## Death Awareness

As we approach sleep, we are naturally reminded of our death. Sleep portends a minideath. Do we trust that a divine presence protects us in the night as well as during the day? Before sleep we turn our heart to God again in prayer, asking for greater trust so that we can let go and, like a child, fall into the arms of our divine Parent.

Our awareness of death need not be morbid or sad. According to a story from the oral tradition of the Desert Fathers and Mothers, an old man was dying in Scete:

> The brothers stood round his bed, and clothed him, and began to weep. But he opened his eyes and began to laugh; it happened three

times. So the brothers asked him: "Tell us, Abba, why do you laugh at our weeping?" And he told them: "I laughed the first time because you fear death; I laughed the second time because you are not ready for death; I laughed the third time, because I am passing from labor to rest, and yet you weep." And so saying, he closed his eyes and died.

Death awareness, or reflection on death and dying, can bring harmony and peace to our life. We tend, however, to avoid thinking about death because we have not come to terms with our fears. As a result, we ignore the limitations of the human body. We fail to acknowledge that death is part of the natural process of life. Religious traditions like Buddhism and Christianity, however, espouse a mindfulness of death. For example, Buddhist monks incorporate meditations on the process of dying into their spiritual practice; and in Christianity, death mindfulness accompanied by belief in the Resurrection can be found throughout the history of the Christian church, beginning with the oral tradition.

With death awareness we acquire a clear sense of priorities. Because we engage in so many activities throughout the day—feeding the children, fulfilling work responsibilities, eating, talking—we can easily lose focus. A simple reflection on death can help us recall the important values of our life and redirect our energy. Knowing that we have a limited time gives us a chance to regain an authentic sense of our relationship with self, others, and God, and places us fully in the moment.

Take some time tonight. Calm yourself, perhaps with a breathing technique, and say to yourself, "I will die." Let that awareness awaken you to the depth of the present moment and perhaps lead to a conversation with yourself on the richness of the day and the people that you are grateful for. Close with this prayer: *Eternal God, grant me an awareness of my death so that I may be open to the true values of my life and learn gratitude for all your blessings. Let me experience my life in a new way through the mindfulness that death is as common as life. May I find strength in the promise of the resurrection.*

## Dreams

Many of us dismiss dreams as unimportant. In our culture we are used to having control over our life. To admit that dreams have any value opens the door to a deeper meaning that weaves its way through our everyday events—a meaning that may challenge us. People in the Scriptures, however, believed that God spoke in dreams, and they called on the power of the unconscious to guide their lives. They were open to the deeper meanings that dreams can reveal.

Some dreams represent unconscious debris of the psyche. Some catch our attention because they carry strong feelings or repeat themselves. The latter kinds of dreams should be listened to. We need to trust the meaning we find in dreams—not the obvious literal meaning but the deeper meaning that is linked to our feelings. Images in dreams tell us one thing on a conscious level, but on a deeper, feeling level, they reveal an entirely different perspective on our lives.

Dreams, like poetry, invite our personal participation. Our interpretations will be unique to our life experience. As symbols, the images, feelings, and people in dreams can be translated on many levels. We should enter the world of the dream and let it speak without imposing a meaning. Our dreams should be translated by us or by someone who knows us well.

Entering the fascinating world of dreams, we uncover threads that guide us in our daily life. God's whispers to us within life events, and dreams tune us in to a message we may not hear in any other way. Like a message in a bottle found on the vast shore of the unconscious, a dream may be God's secret word to us.

## 9. A New Day

When we rise again at the beginning of a new day, we open ourselves to a new life. All around us the world is re-created as birds announce the dawn. We are born again. We have the potential to remain awake to the energy of love that flows through us and through the world—or we can forget the Divine and sleepwalk through the day. The choice is ours.

Ask yourself, In what part of my life do I seem most alive? Begin your practice of mindfulness there. In time you will learn to live out of the ongoing prayer that is already being prayed through you. You will dance and sing in the rhythm of a new song, one that will spring joyfully and spontaneously from the depths of your heart.

> Awake, my soul
> awake, lyre and harp,
> I mean to wake the dawn!
>
> (Psalm 57:8)

# Notes

10  Laurens van der Post, *Jung and the Story of Our Time* (New York: Vintage Books, Random House, 1977), p. 269.

19  Igumen Chariton of Valamo, comp.; E. Kadloubovsky and E. M. Palmer, trans.; Timothy Ware, ed.; *The Art of Prayer: An Orthodox Anthology* (London: Faber and Faber, 1966), p. 119.

20  Abraham Joshua Heschel, *Quest for God: Studies in Prayer and Symbolism* (New York: Crossroad, 1954), p. 8.

21  Kabir Edmund Helminski, *Living Presence: A Sufi Way to Mindfulness and the Essential Self* (New York: G. P. Putnam's Sons, 1992), p. 67.

22  Michael Casey, *The Undivided Heart: The Western Monastic Approach to Contemplation* (Petersham, MA: St. Bede's Publications, 1994), p. 62.

27  Robert Coles, *The Secular Mind* (Princeton, NJ: Princeton University Press, 1999), pp. 32–33.

28  "an upward leap . . ." St. Thérèse of Lisieux, *The Autobiography of St. Thérèse of Lisieux: The Story of a Soul,* translated by John Beevers (Garden City, NY: Image Books, Doubleday and Company, 1957), p. 136.

28  "I keep myself . . ." Brother Lawrence of the Resurrection, *The Practice of the Presence of God,* translated by John J. Delaney (New York: Bantam Doubleday Dell Publishing Group, 1977), p. 68.

30  Igumen Chariton of Valamo, comp.; E. Kadloubovsky
and E. M. Palmer, trans.; Timothy Ware, ed.; *The Art
of Prayer: An Orthodox Anthology* (London: Faber
and Faber, 1966), p. 110.

31–32  James Walsh, ed., *The Cloud of Unknowing*
(Ramsey, NJ: Paulist Press, 1981), pp. 214–215.

36  Jean-Pierre de Caussade, *Abandonment to Divine
Providence,* translated by John Beevers (New York:
Bantam Doubleday Dell Publishing Group, 1975),
p. 51.

37  Martin Buber, *Tales of the Hasidim,* translated by
Olga Marx (New York: Schocken Books, 1947),
p. 173.

40  Igumen Chariton of Valamo, comp.; E. Kadloubovsky
and E. M. Palmer, trans.; Timothy Ware, ed.; *The Art
of Prayer: An Orthodox Anthology* (London: Faber
and Faber, 1966), p. 104.

55  Br. David Steindl-Rast, *Gratefulness, the Heart of
Prayer: An Approach to Life in Fullness* (Ramsey, NJ:
Paulist Press, 1984), pp. 51–52.

58  R. M. French, trans., *The Way of a Pilgrim and The
Pilgrim Continues His Way* (San Francisco: Harper-
SanFrancisco, HarperCollins Publishers, 1965), p. 38.

60  Thomas Keating, *Open Mind, Open Heart* (New
York: Continuum, 1986).

61  Yushi Nomura, *Desert Wisdom: Sayings from the
Desert Fathers* (Garden City, NY: Image Books, by
special arrangement with Doubleday and Company,
1984), p. 59.

73–74  Anthony de Mello, *Taking Flight: A Book of Story Meditations* (New York: Doubleday, Bantam Doubleday Dell Publishing Group, 1990), p. 21.

76  Thich Nhat Hanh, *The Miracle of Mindfulness: A Manual on Meditation,* translated by Mobi Ho (Boston: Beacon Press, 1987), p. 5.

94  "The beginning of our . . ." Abraham Joshua Heschel, *God In Search of Man: A Philosophy of Judaism* (New York: Farrar, Straus and Giroux, 1955), p. 46.

94  "Truly, nothing more . . ." Nikos Kazantzakis, *Report to Greco,* translated by P. A. Bien (New York: Bantam Books, by special arrangement with Simon and Schuster, 1966), p. 40.

107–108  Owen Chadwick, trans., *Western Asceticism* (Philadelphia: Westminster Press, n.d.), p. 140.

# Acknowledgments *(continued)*

The psalms quoted herein are from *Psalms Anew: In Inclusive Language,* compiled by Nancy Schreck and Maureen Leach (Winona, MN: Saint Mary's Press, 1986). Copyright © 1986 by Saint Mary's Press. All rights reserved.

All other scriptural quotations are from the New Revised Standard Version of the Bible. Copyright © 1989 by the Division of Christian Education of the National Council of the Churches of Christ in the United States of America. All rights reserved.

The story from the Jewish mystical tradition on pages 30–31 is adapted from *Gabriel's Palace: Jewish Mystical Tales,* compiled by Howard Schwartz (New York: Oxford University Press, 1993), pages 86–97. Copyright © 1993 by Howard Schwartz. Used by permission of the publisher.

The quotation on page 40 is taken from *The Stream and the Sapphire,* by Denise Levertov (New York: New Directions Publishing Corporation, 1997), page 16. It also appears in *A Door in the Hive.* Copyright © 1989 by Denise Levertov. Reprinted by permission of Gerald Pollinger Ltd., England, and New Directions Publishing Corporation, New York.